MELYNDA HARRISON

Yellowstone Bucket List

50 things to see on your trip to the world's first national park

Copyright © 2023 by Melynda Harrison

All rights reserved. No part of this publication may be reproduced, stored or transmitted in any form or by any means, electronic, mechanical, photocopying, recording, scanning, or otherwise without written permission from the publisher. It is illegal to copy this book, post it to a website, or distribute it by any other means without permission.

Melynda Harrison asserts the moral right to be identified as the author of this work.

Melynda Harrison has no responsibility for the persistence or accuracy of URLs for external or third-party Internet Websites referred to in this publication and does not guarantee that any content on such Websites is, or will remain, accurate or appropriate.

Designations used by companies to distinguish their products are often claimed as trademarks. All brand names and product names used in this book and on its cover are trade names, service marks, trademarks and registered trademarks of their respective owners. The publishers and the book are not associated with any product or vendor mentioned in this book. None of the companies referenced within the book have endorsed the book.

First edition

This book was professionally typeset on Reedsy.
Find out more at reedsy.com

Contents

1	Introduction	1
2	Tips For Visiting Yellowstone - Know Before You Go	4
3	Mammoth Hot Springs Must-Sees	9
4	Tower-Roosevelt and Northeast Must-Sees	13
5	Norris - Madison Must-Sees	17
6	Lower and Midway Geyser Basins Must-Sees	20
7	Old Faithful Area - Lower Geyser Basin Must-Sees	23
8	Yellowstone Lake Must-Sees	28
9	Grand Canyon of the Yellowstone - Hayden Valley Must-Sees	33
10	Three-Day Itinerary	38
11	Six-Day Itinerary	40
12	Conclusion	43

1

Introduction

The first time I was supposed to visit Yellowstone National Park, I was 15 years old. My uncle offered to take my brother and me on a trip to this iconic park. But in the summer of 1988, huge wildfires raged across Yellowstone, the results of which can still be seen today, and our trip was canceled.

Fast forward to 1994. I was a national exchange student at the University of Montana in Missoula. A group of friends and I drove four hours on winter roads to the North Entrance of Yellowstone. We passed beneath the Roosevelt Arch and cross-country skied along the Blacktail Plateau Ski Trail. That February night was camped in the Mammoth Campground ...and it was freezing! We skied again the next day and got a hotel room that night in the cozy Mammoth Hotel.

That introduction to Wonderland stuck with me and like a magnet, pulled me back again and again.

In graduate school, I researched and wrote about the natural history of the Greater Yellowstone Ecoregion. Living in Jackson, Wyoming I got into the park whenever I could. When I moved to Montana, I worked as an outdoor educator in Yellowstone, a natural history and wildlife-watching guide, and wrote articles about visiting the park for regional and national magazines.

Now I run a website (YellowstoneTrips.com) and Facebook group (facebook.com/groups/YellowstoneTrips) dedicated to helping people plan their Yellowstone trips.

I've been interviewed by National Geographic and Samantha Brown, and been a guest on numerous podcasts, talking about Yellowstone and Montana. And of course, I get into the park as often as I can for my enjoyment.

Exploring Yellowstone and raising my kids here has given me so much joy and I want to share that with you.

This book provides a curated list of 50 must-see attractions in Yellowstone National Park, offering you an inspirational and immersive journey through the park's diverse landscapes. It serves as a guide for first-time visitors and returning enthusiasts seeking expert recommendations.

This book is not a total planning guide, but inspiration. I want you to be excited about your trip to Yellowstone and feel like you have a few places you want to see, and a few experiences you want to have, and then be open to spontaneous adventures.

I started my Facebook group to help people plan their travels to Yellowstone and Glacier National Parks and the rest of Montana. The number one question in that group is "What are the must-sees in Yellowstone?" This book is my attempt to answer that question.

INTRODUCTION

* * *

How To Use This Book

This book is organized geographically so you can find the must-sees in each section of the park. I start with some tips to help make your trip as easy, fun, and as exciting as possible and then jump right into the 50 places and experiences you don't want to miss in Yellowstone.

This isn't necessarily a book you will read from cover to cover, though you could. I imagine you leafing through it and seeing what catches your imagination. Or check out the geographical location you are planning to visit and choose a few key must-sees.

This also isn't a definitive planning guide (I have a website for that, remember?), but I hope this little book will get you excited and make sure you don't miss the main "attractions" that make a Yellowstone visit so special.

CAVEAT

You won't be able to see all 50 of these items in one trip to Yellowstone nor should you try. This is a fun way to see what's out there, but it would be a shame to spend your time in Yellowstone running from one thing to another just to check them off your list. Use this as a reminder that there are always more things to see and do!

2

Tips For Visiting Yellowstone - Know Before You Go

Wolf in the Lamar Valley – seen through a telephoto lens.

Wildlife Watching Tips

Respect Wildlife Distances

Maintain a safe distance from wildlife. Use binoculars or a telephoto lens to get a closer look without disturbing their natural behavior.

Approaching on foot within 100 yards of bears or wolves or 25 yards of other wildlife is prohibited by the National Park Service and common sense. Do not stop in the road to look at animals or take photos use roadside pullouts, and if there isn't one, keep going.

Use Quiet Observation Techniques

Keep noise to a minimum. Silence your phone, speak in hushed tones, and move slowly to avoid startling animals when viewing from a safe distance. Other times it's good to let an animal know you are there so you don't startle it.

Dawn and Dusk are Prime Times

Wildlife is most active during the early morning and late evening. Plan your wildlife-watching excursions during these times for optimal sightings. You will see critters at all hours of the day, especially elk, bison, coyotes, and birds, but dawn and dusk are best.

Stay on Designated Trails

Respect trail guidelines. Venturing off-trail can disrupt fragile habitats and increase the risk of wildlife encounters. Most people get great photos from the road, next to their car.

Educate Yourself on Wildlife Behavior

Understanding animal behavior enhances your experience and ensures safety. Learn about the species you might encounter. Check with the rangers in the visitor centers to learn how to be a responsible wildlife watcher. The park newspaper also has good tips and explains the park regulations.

Photography Tips

Golden Hour Magic

Capture the park's beauty during the golden hours—the hour after sunrise and before sunset—for soft, warm lighting. Blue hour — 20-30 minutes before sunrise and after sunset —can be nice too.

Bring a Variety of Lenses

Pack a versatile set of lenses to capture diverse scenes. A wide-angle lens is great for landscapes, while a telephoto lens is essential for wildlife photography. If you don't have a fancy camera and multiple lenses, you can still get great photos with your phone, but some wildlife may be too far away to capture without a telephoto lens.

Patience is Key

Wait for the perfect moment. Patience often yields remarkable shots of wildlife engaging in natural behaviors.

Utilize Natural Framing

Incorporate natural elements like trees or rock formations to frame your subject and add depth to your photographs.

Experiment with Composition

Play with composition techniques such as leading lines, the rule of thirds, and framing to create visually striking images.

Hiking Tips

Check Trail Conditions

Before embarking on a hike, check trail conditions and closures. Yellowstone's weather can vary, and trails may be impacted. Sometimes trails are closed due to bear activity or for other reasons.

Carry Bear Spray

In bear country, it's essential to carry bear spray and know how to use it. Make noise while hiking to alert bears to your presence.

Dress in Layers

Weather in Yellowstone can change rapidly. Dress in layers to adapt to temperature fluctuations throughout the day.

Hydrate and Pack Snacks

Stay hydrated, especially at higher elevations (and it might all be higher elevation depending on where you are coming from). Carry water and energy-boosting snacks to fuel your hikes.

Inform Someone of Your Plans

Before setting out on a hike, inform someone of your itinerary. This ensures someone knows your whereabouts in case of an emergency.

3

Mammoth Hot Springs Must-Sees

Mammoth Terraces

1. Roosevelt Arch

Standing proudly at the North Entrance of Yellowstone National Park, the Roosevelt Arch is an iconic symbol of the park's grandeur. Constructed in 1903, this colossal stone arch welcomes visitors with the inscription "For the Benefit and Enjoyment of the People," a testament to the park's dedication to preserving natural beauty. The arch frames the stunning landscape beyond, inviting adventurers to embark on a journey into the heart of Yellowstone.

2. Mammoth Hot Springs Elk

Mammoth Hot Springs is not only renowned for its geological wonders but also for the enchanting wildlife that graces its landscapes. The Mammoth Hot Springs elk, in particular, add a majestic touch to the scene. Often spotted grazing near the hotel and on the Parade Grounds, these elegant creatures become part of the park's living tapestry. They are still wild animals, so keep your distance.

3. Fort Yellowstone and the Army Era

Immerse yourself in the history of Yellowstone at Fort Yellowstone, a historic military outpost that played a vital role in the park's early years. Built during the Army Era in the late 19th and early 20th centuries, the fort served as a base for the troops assigned to protect Yellowstone's natural resources. Today, visitors can explore the remnants of this fascinating chapter in the park's history, including the Mammoth Hot Springs Historic District. Grab a pamphlet at the visitor center and take a self-guided tour.

4. Mammoth Hot Springs Terraces

MAMMOTH HOT SPRINGS MUST-SEES

One of Yellowstone's most captivating geological features, the Mammoth Hot Springs Terraces, creates a surreal landscape of travertine terraces formed by the flow of hot water laden with minerals. This hot spring area is different than the other hot spring basins in the park because the underlying rock here is limestone. The rest of the park is mostly volcanic rhyolite, the lava form of granite. The terraces are an ever-changing display of intricate formations, cascading pools, and vibrant colors.

5. The Hoodoos

The Yellowstone Hoodoos aren't like the ones you see in Bryce Canyon; rather than pinnacles of weathered sandstone, they are travertine stacks from Terrace Mountain. Start at the Glen Creek Trailhead and follow the signs at each junction. The trail is about 3 miles one-way (to the Upper Terraces) and has views of Bunsen Peak, wildflowers in season, and jumbles of rocks to climb about on.

6. Osprey Falls Overlook

For those seeking breathtaking views and a touch of adventure, the Osprey Falls Overlook is a must-visit destination. A hike to the overlook rewards visitors with a view of 150-foot Osprey Falls and the surrounding Sheepeater Canyon - one of the deepest canyons in Yellowstone. The thundering cascade and the rugged beauty of the canyon create a mesmerizing scene, making this overlook a prime spot for both nature lovers and avid photographers looking to capture the untamed essence of Yellowstone. Park at the Bunsen Peak Trailhead and follow Old Bunsen Peak Road 3 miles to Osprey Falls Trail. Descend 700 feet into the canyon.

7. Bunsen Peak

Bunsen Peak offers a challenging yet rewarding hike, promising unparalleled views of the surrounding landscape. Named after the renowned scientist Robert Bunsen who invented the Bunsen Burner and studied geysers, this peak provides a vantage point to appreciate the vastness of Yellowstone. The trail winds through diverse ecosystems, from sagebrush to sparse forest, to a rocky top, offering glimpses of wildlife and wildflowers. At the summit, hikers are treated to a 360-degree panorama of Mammoth Hot Springs, Blacktail Plateau, Swan Lake Flats, and more. The trail is 2.1 miles and 1,300 feet one-way.

4

Tower-Roosevelt and Northeast Must-Sees

Tower Fall

8. Undine Falls

Nestled along the scenic route between Mammoth Hot Springs and Tower-Roosevelt, Undine Falls captivates visitors with its graceful descent. Named after the mythical water nymphs, the falls cascade over a series of rocky steps, creating a mesmerizing spectacle. The vantage point near Undine Falls offers a serene atmosphere and it's just steps from a pullout, making it a quick, easy stop. You can also hike around to the other side of the falls from the Lava Creek Trail.

9. Petrified Trees

Located in the Northern Range, the petrified trees are remnants of an ancient forest that existed over 50 million years ago. Fossilized and preserved, these trees stand as silent witnesses to the geological transformations that have shaped the landscape. The Petrified Tree is a weird exhibit, in my opinion. It looks like a tree stump and is surrounded by a black, iron fence. But, if you know the history – that it is a Redwood tree from tens of millions of years ago, it's pretty interesting. You'll find it on a signed spur road 1.3 miles west of Tower Junction. However, there are other ways to see petrified trees in Yellowstone. The Petrified Trees of Specimen Ridge day hike starts in a pullout 4.5 miles from Tower Junction toward the North East Entrance and just before the Lamar River Bridge. An unmarked, unmaintained trail leads to the top of Specimen Ridge in about 1.5 miles each way. *Remember, it is illegal to remove any features from the park, including petrified wood.

10. Western Chuck Wagon Dinner

Immerse yourself in the Old West charm and culinary delights. The Old West Dinner Cookout starts with a scenic wagon ride from Roosevelt

Corrals that provides a glimpse into Yellowstone's history and its cowboy heritage. Guests can savor traditional Western fare while surrounded by the park's stunning natural beauty. Expect grilled meats, cornbread, and beans with a memorable blend of history, song, and hospitality under the expansive sky.

11. Calcite Springs Overlook

Perched above the Yellowstone River, the Calcite Springs Overlook offers a view of the rugged Grand Canyon of the Yellowstone below. The overlook provides a glimpse into the geothermal features of the area, with steam rising from the hydrothermal vents along the riverbanks. The contrast between the steaming banks and the river's pristine beauty creates a captivating scene.

12. Tower Fall

One of Yellowstone's most iconic waterfalls, Tower Fall plunges dramatically into the Tower Creek Canyon. Accessible via a short trail, the viewpoint near the falls allows visitors to witness the majestic cascade framed by towering cliffs. Tower Fall is not only a spectacle of nature but also a place with historical significance, as the 1870 Washburn-Langford-Doane Expedition named it. The beauty and accessibility of Tower Fall make it a must-see destination for those exploring the northeastern reaches of the park. Be sure to grab ice cream in the general store while you are there.

13. Mount Washburn Summit

For panoramic views and a sense of accomplishment, venture to the Mount Washburn Summit. Standing at an elevation of over 10,000 feet, this prominent peak offers a bird's-eye perspective of Yellowstone and even the Grand Tetons on a clear day. The trail to the summit climbs steadily and provides opportunities to encounter wildlife, especially mountain goats. Once atop Mount Washburn, hikers are rewarded with unparalleled vistas of the surrounding mountains, canyons, and geothermal features from the fire lookout. There is an enclosed area with a viewing telescope, bench seating, and interpretive information inside the lookout station. Start from Chittenden Road Trailhead for the shortest route — 2.8 miles one-way and 1,500 feet elevation gain.

14. Lamar Valley Wildlife Watching

Renowned as the "Serengeti of North America," Lamar Valley is a wildlife lover's paradise. This expansive valley provides prime habitat for a diverse array of animals, including bison, elk, wolves, and grizzlies. The wide-open spaces and meandering Lamar River create optimal conditions for wildlife viewing. Visitors can embark on a wildlife-watching adventure, keeping a keen eye out for the fascinating behaviors of Yellowstone's resident fauna against the backdrop of the valley's picturesque landscapes. Look for people standing around spotting scopes or book a wildlife-watching tour for the best chance of seeing critters.

15. Trout Lake

Tucked away in the northeastern corner of the park, Trout Lake offers a serene escape surrounded by forest, meadows, and pristine waters. The lake is a favorite among nature lovers, with opportunities for hiking and wildflower observation. In early July, trout spawn up the inlet stream and you will often see otters and bald eagles hunting the fish.

5

Norris - Madison Must-Sees

Norris Geyser Basin

16. Obsidian Cliff

Steeped in geological marvels, Obsidian Cliff stands as a testament to Yellowstone's fiery origins. Located between Mammoth Hot Springs and Norris Geyser Basin, this towering formation is composed almost entirely of obsidian, a volcanic glass formed during ancient volcanic activity. Visitors can explore the base of the cliff, marveling at the columnar rock formations and imagining the volcanic forces that shaped this extraordinary feature. The kiosk at Obsidian Cliff, constructed in 1931, was the first wayside exhibit in a US national park. *Remember, it is illegal to remove any features from the park, including obsidian.

17. Norris Geyser Basin

Norris Geyser Basin, located at the intersection of the park's two major fault lines, is a dynamic thermal area. Home to the park's hottest and most acidic geothermal features, Norris captivates visitors with its otherworldly landscapes. The basin features a variety of geysers, hot springs, and fumaroles, each with its distinct character. Norris Geyser Basin is home to Steamboat Geyser with the highest eruption flume in Yellowstone, but it erupts only occasionally and with no way to predict when it will happen. The visitor center was constructed by the CCC in classic "parketecture."

18. Museum of the National Park Ranger

Immerse yourself in the rich history of park rangers and their role in preserving America's natural treasures at the Museum of the National Park Ranger. Located across the road from Norris Geyser Basin, the museum provides insight into the evolution of the National Park Service and the dedicated individuals who have safeguarded Yellowstone. Exhibits showcase the tools, uniforms, and stories of park rangers throughout the years, offering a comprehensive look at the challenges and triumphs of protecting these pristine landscapes. For those with a passion for conservation and the outdoors, the museum serves as a compelling tribute to the men and women who have played a vital role in preserving the nation's natural heritage.

19. Artists Paint Pots

Artists Paint Pots is a geothermal wonderland that captivates visitors with its vibrant and dynamic features. The bubbling mud pots and colorful hot springs create an artistic display that inspired the name of this unique thermal area. Visitors can follow a short trail to witness the rhythmic gurgling and splattering of the mud pots, creating a sensory experience that combines sight and sound. The ever-changing nature of Artists Paint Pots, with its playful bursts of activity, makes it a must-see destination for those seeking the artistic expressions of Yellowstone's geothermal wonders.

6

Lower and Midway Geyser Basins Must-Sees

Grand Prismatic Hot Spring

20. Firehole River Swimming Hole

The Firehole River Swimming Hole in Firehole Canyon offers a refreshing and unique experience for Yellowstone visitors. The river, known for its warm waters due to the geothermal activity in the area, creates a natural swimming hole that beckons those seeking a cooling escape. It's the only place in the park where you can swim in hot spring water, however, it is more warm than hot. It's closed during high water, so check with the Park Service before planning your plunge.

21. Fountain Paint Pot

Located in the Lower Geyser Basin, Fountain Paint Pot is a geothermal feature that showcases the dynamic and artistic side of Yellowstone's hydrothermal activity. The bubbling mud pots, fumaroles, and vibrant hot springs create a symphony of colors and textures. Visitors can stroll along the boardwalk, observing the playful antics of the mud pots as they erupt and spatter. The unique combination of the bubbling mud and the vivid hues of thermophiles makes Fountain Paint Pot a captivating stop.

22. Grand Prismatic Spring

As one of Yellowstone's most well-known features, the Grand Prismatic Spring in the Midway Geyser Basin is a mesmerizing display of vibrant colors and thermal energy. This is the hot spring on the cover of this book and the one you see in aerial view all the time. The spring's vivid hues, ranging from deep blues to fiery oranges, create a surreal landscape that is best viewed from the overlook on Fairy Falls Trail. The boardwalk view is lovely but not quite as stunning as from above. The microbial mats surrounding the spring contribute to its striking palette. Grand Prismatic Spring is the largest hot spring in the United States.

23. Fairy Falls Trail

For those seeking a blend of natural beauty and adventure, the Fairy Falls Trail offers a scenic journey to the breathtaking Fairy Falls. Located in the Midway Geyser Basin, the trail winds through a picturesque forest and opens up to expansive meadows. Hikers are rewarded with panoramic views of the surrounding landscape and glimpses of iconic features like Grand Prismatic Spring. The trail culminates at the base of the enchanting Fairy Falls, where a cascade of water plunges gracefully into a serene pool. The Fairy Falls Trail provides an immersive experience, combining the allure of Yellowstone's geothermal wonders with the tranquility of its lush wilderness.

7

Old Faithful Area - Lower Geyser Basin Must-Sees

Old Faithful Geyser

24. Old Faithful Geyser

Old Faithful Geyser, an enduring symbol of Yellowstone, captivates visitors with its (somewhat) predictable and powerful eruptions. Located in the Upper Geyser Basin, Old Faithful spouts boiling water into the air approximately every 90 minutes. The surrounding area, known as the Old Faithful Historic District, features a visitor center and multiple vantage points for optimal viewing. Visitors gather around the geyser, eagerly anticipating the spectacular display, making Old Faithful an iconic and must-see attraction in Yellowstone National Park. Check the visitor center or hotel for predicted eruption times.

25. Upper Geyser Basin Boardwalks

The Upper Geyser Basin boasts the highest concentration of geysers globally, and the extensive boardwalk system allows you to explore this unique landscape safely. Pick up an interpretive brochure and wind through a surreal terrain of erupting geysers, bubbling hot springs, and colorful microbial mats. The boardwalks provide an intimate and immersive experience with Yellowstone's hydrothermal features. Each step offers a sensory journey, from the hissing steam to the vibrant hues of the thermophiles, making the Upper Geyser Basin Boardwalks an essential exploration for those fascinated by the park's geological wonders.

26. Old Faithful Inn

A masterpiece of rustic architecture, Old Faithful Inn stands as a testament to the early days of park tourism. Located near the famous geyser, the inn is a historic building that exudes charm and grandeur. Constructed with local materials like lodgepole pine and rhyolite stone, the inn's design harmonizes with its natural surroundings. Visitors can marvel at the towering lobby, adorned with a massive stone fireplace, and stay in rooms that blend historic charm with modern comfort. Old Faithful Inn offers a unique lodging experience, allowing guests to immerse themselves in the park's history while enjoying the convenience of proximity to the iconic Old Faithful Geyser. You don't have to stay there to enjoy it. Wander through the lobby on your own or attend one of the several tours given daily.

27. Yellowstone Tribal Heritage Center

The Yellowstone Tribal Heritage Center honors the rich and diverse heritage of the region's indigenous peoples. This center serves as a gateway to understanding the deep connections between the land and the Indigenous communities that have thrived in the Yellowstone ecosystem for generations. Members of the 27 associated Tribes of Yellowstone National Park interact with visitors through formal and informal education. Artifacts, storytelling, and multimedia presentations weave a narrative that transcends centuries, offering a profound appreciation for the deep cultural significance of Yellowstone. As a tribute to the enduring legacy of Indigenous communities, the center fosters a greater understanding of the symbiotic relationship between nature and the people who have called this land home for centuries.

28. Bike to Morning Glory Pool

There aren't a lot of places in Yellowstone where biking is allowed, so biking to Morning Glory Pool provides something a little different and a scenic journey. The trailhead begins at the Old Faithful area, passing hot springs to reach the vibrant and aptly named Morning Glory Pool, making it a rewarding and active way to appreciate one of Yellowstone's renowned thermal features. Rent bikes at the Bear's Den in the Old Faithful Snow Lodge or bring your own.

29. Lone Star Geyser Trail

Embark on a serene hike (or bike ride) along the Lone Star Geyser Trail, offering a peaceful escape into Yellowstone's backcountry. Accessible from the Old Faithful area or the Lone Star Geyser Trailhead, the trail meanders through pine forests and open meadows, eventually leading to the Lone Star Geyser. This trail is a lesser-known gem, providing a more secluded experience compared to the crowded boardwalks. Hikers are rewarded with the rhythmic eruptions of Lone Star Geyser against the backdrop of pristine wilderness.

30. Kepler Cascades

Situated along the Firehole River at the trailhead for Lone Star Geyser is a captivating display of cascading water. Easily accessible from the main road and viewed from a bridge, this picturesque waterfall delights visitors with its graceful descent over rugged rocks, creating a symphony of sounds that harmonize with the surrounding natural beauty.

31. Continental Divide / Isa Lake

Discover the geographical heart of North America at the Continental Divide in Yellowstone. Here the waters part, flowing either west to the Pacific Ocean or east to the Atlantic Ocean. Isa Lake, nestled along the divide, is a cute little pond that marks this unique hydrological crossroads. Visitors can appreciate the significance of this natural divide and the serene beauty of Isa Lake, making it a tranquil stop for those traversing the Continental Divide twice between Old Faithful and West

Thumb Geyser Basins. The location offers a profound reminder of the park's role in shaping the continent's watershed.

8

Yellowstone Lake Must-Sees

West Thumb Geyser Basin and Yellowstone Lake

32. West Thumb Geyser Basin

The West Thumb Geyser Basin offers a mesmerizing blend of geothermal wonders and the tranquil beauty of Yellowstone Lake. Situated on the shores of the lake, this area features hot springs, geysers, and bubbling pools, creating a surreal landscape against the backdrop of the expansive lake. Visitors can stroll along the boardwalks, marveling at the geothermal features while enjoying breathtaking views of Yellowstone Lake and the surrounding mountains. Look for Abyss Pool — darkly colored and one of the deepest in the basin, and Fishing Cone where early visitors to the park were said to catch fish in the lake and cook them on the line over the vent.

33. Hike to Heart Lake

Embark on a picturesque journey through Yellowstone's backcountry with the hike to Heart Lake. Accessible from the Heart Lake Trailhead, this lengthy trek takes hikers through thin forests and open meadows along a fairly flat trail. The destination, Heart Lake, is a pristine and secluded gem nestled in a wild basin under steep mountains. The hike provides opportunities for wildlife encounters, passes backcountry hot springs, and offers a sense of solitude as visitors reach the shores of the lake. The trail is 7.5 miles one-way and has little elevation gain or loss. The mosquitoes can be relentless.

34. Lake Hotel

Elegance meets wilderness at the historic Lake Hotel, a refined retreat on the shores of Yellowstone Lake. Dating back to 1891, the hotel exudes Old World charm and provides guests with a luxurious base for exploring the park. The colonial-style architecture, expansive verandas, and sweeping views of Yellowstone Lake create an atmosphere of timeless sophistication. Guests can unwind in comfortable rooms adorned with period furnishings, dine in the acclaimed Lake Yellowstone Hotel Dining Room, and savor the unique blend of luxury and natural beauty that defines this iconic Yellowstone accommodation. You don't have to stay there to enjoy a drink and piano music in the lobby with a view of the beautiful lake.

35. Elephant Back Trail

For panoramic vistas and a moderately challenging hike, the Elephant Back Trail between Fishing Bridge and Lake Lodge is an ideal choice. The trail leads hikers through dense forests to a ridge that offers stunning views of Yellowstone Lake and the surrounding mountains. Named for its distinctive shape resembling an elephant's back, this trail provides a rewarding outdoor experience without an overly strenuous ascent. The trail is a 5.2-mile lollipop loop.

36. Natural Bridge Trail

Experience the wonders of erosion and geology along the Natural Bridge Trail near Bridge Bay. This short and accessible trail takes visitors to a natural bridge—a rock formation sculpted by the erosive forces of water. The trail winds through a pine forest, and as visitors approach the natural bridge, they are treated to a captivating display of nature's artistry. The Natural Bridge Trail is an easy 1-mile one-way trail.

37. Scenic Cruise on Yellowstone Lake

Indulge in the beauty of Yellowstone Lake with a scenic cruise, an enchanting way to explore the park's largest body of water. Departing from Bridge Bay Marina, the cruise takes passengers on a journey across the ocean-like lake, offering unobstructed views of the surrounding mountains and the vast wilderness. As the boat glides over the sometimes rough water, passengers learn about the lake's geological and ecological significance. A scenic cruise on Yellowstone Lake provides a unique perspective and an opportunity to appreciate the park's natural beauty from a different vantage point.

38. Fishing Bridge

Spanning the Yellowstone River where it flows out of Yellowstone Lake, Fishing Bridge offers views of the Yellowstone River. Fishing Bridge is renowned for its wildlife viewing opportunities, and visitors often spot trout and other aquatic species from the bridge. The nearby campground, store, and visitor center make Fishing Bridge a central hub for those exploring the eastern side of Yellowstone.

39. Pelican Valley Bird Watching

Wetland areas, such as where Pelican Creek flows into Yellowstone Lake, are havens for birdwatchers seeking a diverse array of avian species. The nutrient-rich waters attract wading birds like avocets, black-necked stilts, and the occasional great blue heron. Witness the captivating water-walking display of Western grebes, adding to the avian spectacle. Birdwatching in Pelican Valley provides a peaceful and immersive experience. The Pelican Creek Nature Trail is a 0.06-mile loop that will get you into the good stuff.

40. Avalanche Peak Trail

For those seeking a challenging hike and breathtaking panoramic views, the Avalanche Peak Trail is a must-try adventure near Lake Village. The trail ascends through alpine meadows and rocky slopes to the summit of Avalanche Peak, offering hikers a sense of accomplishment and awe-inspiring vistas of Yellowstone Lake and surrounding mountain ranges. The trail is known for its wildflower displays during the summer months, adding a burst of color to the rugged terrain. Avalanche Peak Trail is short and steep — 2,100 feet in 2.1 miles one-way.

9

Grand Canyon of the Yellowstone - Hayden Valley Must-Sees

Lower Falls of the Yellowstone

41. Virginia Cascades

Virginia Cascades is a picturesque waterfall located on Virginia Cascade Drive, a 3-mile one-way scenic drive between Norris and Canyon Village. The cascade is a 60-foot drop of the Gibbon River over rugged rocks. Surrounded by dense forest, the falls offer a tranquil escape.

42. Cascade Lake

Tucked away beneath Observation Peak, Cascade Lake is a quiet, often marshy, lake accessible via the Cascade Lake Trail. The trail winds through mixed coniferous forests and low, open meadows, providing hikers with glimpses of diverse ecosystems. As you approach the 36-acre Cascade Lake the water is surrounded by tall grass and rolling hills. Cascade Lake offers good fishing for Yellowstone cutthroat trout and Arctic grayling. The trail is 2.25 miles one-way and mostly flat.

43. Brink of the Upper Falls

Stand on the brink of thundering waters at the Brink of the Upper Falls, a dramatic viewpoint along the Grand Canyon of the Yellowstone River. Accessible via a short but steep hike, this vantage point offers a close-up encounter with the Yellowstone River as it plunges over the Upper Falls. The roar of the cascading water and the spray in the air create a sensory experience, allowing visitors to appreciate the raw power of nature. The Brink of the Upper Falls is a good spot to access the North Rim Trail that follows the canyon to Inspiration Point.

44. Brink of the Lower Falls

Perched on the edge of the Grand Canyon of the Yellowstone, the Brink of the Lower Falls provides an awe-inspiring view of the Yellowstone River as it hurtles over the Lower Falls. Reached by a well-maintained trail, this viewpoint offers a breathtaking perspective of the thundering waterfall and the canyon's vibrant colors. The mist from the falls adds a refreshing touch to the experience. The Brink of the Lower Falls is well worth the effort to get down there (and back up) and there are benches along the way if you need a rest.

45. Lookout Point

Immerse yourself in the grandeur of the Grand Canyon of the Yellowstone at Lookout Point, a scenic overlook that provides breathtaking views of the canyon and the Lower Falls. The viewpoint is easily accessible, allowing visitors to marvel at the canyon's colorful rock walls and the river's turbulent descent. Keep an eye out for osprey circling above the river and nesting on the pinnacles of the canyon. Lookout Point is a prime location for capturing the sheer magnitude and beauty of Yellowstone's iconic canyon landscape.

46. Inspiration Point

True to its name, Inspiration Point offers a visually striking panorama of the Grand Canyon of the Yellowstone. Accessible via a short hike, this viewpoint provides a commanding perspective of the canyon's vibrant hues and the meandering Yellowstone River below. The juxtaposition of the colorful canyon walls and the surrounding forest creates a scene that has inspired generations of Yellowstone visitors. Inspiration Point is a perfect spot for contemplation, photography, and connecting with the awe-inspiring beauty of the park's geological wonders. This is also a good spot to access the North Rim Trail that follows the edge of the canyon to the Brink of the Upper Falls.

47. Artist Point

Renowned as one of the most photographed locations in Yellowstone, Artist Point is a captivating viewpoint that showcases the grandeur of the Grand Canyon of the Yellowstone. Perched on the south rim, this overlook offers an unobstructed view of the Lower Falls, framed by the colorful canyon walls. The scene is reminiscent of a painted masterpiece, and it's easy to understand why this location earned its artistic moniker. Whether capturing the changing colors of the canyon during sunrise or witnessing the soft hues of sunset, Artist Point is a must-visit destination for photographers and admirers of Yellowstone's natural beauty. To get away from the crowds, take a walk along the Ribbon Lake Trail which leaves from here.

48. Hayden Valley Bison Herd

Hayden Valley is a wildlife enthusiast's paradise, and one of its most iconic inhabitants is the Hayden Valley bison herd. Roaming the expansive meadows and riverbanks, these majestic creatures contribute to the timeless charm of Yellowstone. Visitors can witness the bison's iconic presence, whether grazing peacefully, crossing the Yellowstone River, or causing a bison jam and holding up traffic. The Hayden Valley bison are a living symbol of the park's commitment to preserving the natural behaviors of its wildlife, providing a captivating and authentic experience for those exploring Yellowstone's vast landscapes. You may also see wolves and a plethora of bird life.

49. LeHardy Rapids

Nestled along the Yellowstone River, LeHardy Rapids is a dynamic and scenic location where the river rushes over rocky terrain, creating frothy rapids and cascades. Accessible via the LeHardy Rapids Picnic Area, visitors can enjoy a peaceful spot for a picnic while marveling at the river's lively display. The location is named after early Yellowstone photographer and pioneer Charles LeHardy, adding a historical touch to the natural beauty of the area. LeHardy Rapids is a serene stop for those seeking a riverside escape and the soothing sounds of rushing water as well as a stellar waterfowl-watching spot. In late spring you may see Yellowstone cutthroat trout leaping upstream and Harlequin ducks.

50. Mud Volcano

Step into a surreal landscape at Mud Volcano, an area in Hayden Valley known for its hydrothermal features and bubbling mud pots. The geothermal activity, including churning mud and vibrant thermophiles, creates a fascinating and otherworldly scene. The Dragon's Mouth Spring, part of Mud Volcano, emits steam and roars like a mythical creature, adding to the area's mystique. Boardwalks guide visitors through the geothermal features, allowing them to witness the raw power and unpredictability of Yellowstone's subterranean forces. Be sure to cross the street to see Sulphur Cauldron. Mud Volcano is one of the more sulfur-smelling areas in the park.

10

Three-Day Itinerary

The three-day itinerary assumes you are staying in West Yellowstone, Montana.

The three days of touring are in no particular order, so mix them up as you see fit. If you are leaving through the South Entrance, make Day Two your last day. If you are leaving through the East Entrance, Day One or Two should be your final day in the park.

Day 1: West Yellowstone – Old Faithful Area

- Firehole Canyon Drive
- Old Faithful Area
- Kepler Cascades
- West Thumb
- Midway Geyser Basin
- Fountain Paint Pots

Day 2: West Yellowstone –Norris – Canyon

- Norris Geyser Basin
- Virginia Cascade
- Grand Canyon of the Yellowstone

Day 3: West Yellowstone – Mammoth

- Artists Paintpots
- Mammoth Visitor Education Center
- Fort Yellowstone Walking Tour
- Mammoth Terraces
- Roosevelt Arch
- Gibbon Falls

11

Six-Day Itinerary

With the six-day itinerary, you'll stay in West Yellowstone, Montana for two nights, Roosevelt Lodge Cabins for two nights, and Chico Hot Springs in the Paradise Valley, Montana for one night.

Flying in and out of Bozeman, Montana makes the most sense for this itinerary.

Day 1: Bozeman - West Yellowstone - Norris

- West Yellowstone Visitor Information Center
- Artists Paintpots
- Norris Geyser Basin
- Gibbon Falls
- Overnight in West Yellowstone

Day 2: West Yellowstone - Old Faithful Area

- Firehole Canyon Drive

- Old Faithful Area
- Kepler Cascades
- West Thumb
- Midway Geyser Basin
- Fountain Paint Pots
- Overnight in West Yellowstone

Day 3: West Yellowstone - Canyon - Roosevelt

- Virginia Cascade
- Grand Canyon of the Yellowstone
- Mount Washburn
- Tower Falls
- Overnight at Roosevelt Lodge Cabins

Day 4: Roosevelt -Lamar Valley

- Wildlife Watching in Lamar
- Trout Lake
- Barronette Peak Overlook
- Pebble Creek Canyon
- Silvergate, MT
- Wildlife Watching in Lamar
- Overnight At Roosevelt Lodge Cabins

Day 5: Roosevelt - Mammoth - Chico Hot Springs

- Undine Falls

- Mammoth Visitor Education Center
- Fort Yellowstone Walking Tour
- Mammoth Terraces
- Roosevelt Arch
- Overnight at Chico Hot Springs

Day 6: Chico Hot Springs - Bozeman

- Chico Hot Springs
- Pine Creek Falls Hike

12

Conclusion

There you go! 50 awesome places and experiences in Yellowstone National Park. From geysers to waterfalls to incredible hikes, I hope this provides inspiration for your trip or functions as a small guide while you are here.

If you want more planning resources, please see my website: YellowstoneTrips.com. And sign up for my monthly email there, where I get deep into Yellowstone as well as my other travels.

If you've found this book helpful, I'd be very appreciative if you left a favorable review on Amazon.

Made in United States
Orlando, FL
11 February 2025